THE SOUL AND IT'S TRUE NATURE

(BASED ON BHAGAVAD GITA'S 2ND CHAPTER)

DR. JAGADEESH PILLAI

Copyright © Dr. Jagadeesh Pillai
All Rights Reserved.

This book has been published with all efforts taken to make the material error-free after the consent of the author. However, the author and the publisher do not assume and hereby disclaim any liability to any party for any loss, damage, or disruption caused by errors or omissions, whether such errors or omissions result from negligence, accident, or any other cause.

While every effort has been made to avoid any mistake or omission, this publication is being sold on the condition and understanding that neither the author nor the publishers or printers would be liable in any manner to any person by reason of any mistake or omission in this publication or for any action taken or omitted to be taken or advice rendered or accepted on the basis of this work. For any defect in printing or binding the publishers will be liable only to replace the defective copy by another copy of this work then available.

|| *Dedicated to all those Souls who are in despondency* ||

Contents

Prayer

HARE RAMA HARE RAMA, RAMA RAMA HARE HARE
- HARE KRISHNA, HARE KRISHNA, KRISHNA
KRISHNA, HARE HARE

(Mantra - Kali Santaranopanishad)

Preface

Before entering into the teaching of this chapter, for an in-depth and easy understanding of it, let us try to understand the "Krishna & Arjuna" one again.

In this chapter onwards, Krishna enters with his teachings. So, who is Krishna?

Throughout all the next chapters at most of the places, Krishna will explain to him as the CREATOR of everything....."THE SUPREME SPIRIT".

So here the teacher is "KRISHNA", "The Creator", "The Supreme Spirit", "Parabrahma" etc.

ARJUNA - as mentioned in the previous chapter, represents we human beings. However, a human is not just a BODY, but a Human is a Body with Soul. Without a soul, it's like a DEAD BODY. When a woman or mother conceives two cells, literally a meatball only creates. Somewhere between 40 to 48 days after conception, the soul enters and the life process starts.

When the soul, which has all the powers, enters the body, then onwards only the human reacts and does all the actions.

And the SOUL (Jeevatma) is a part of the "SUPREME SPIRIT" (Paramatma) – its divine.

We, humans, have no control over it, rather Soul &

Supreme controls us.

Because of this SOUL, we have MIND AND SENSES.

The actions of Mind and Senses reflect in our life.

When the mind is happy, we are happy and when the mind is sad, we are unhappy.

In Bhagavad Gita, the talk is between **KRISHNA and ARJUNA**.

Krishna represents "SUPREME SPIRIT"

Arjuna represents "A SOUL with Mind and Senses".

Krishna & Arjuna – the names resemble human form just for our understanding.

Since the mind is responsible for everything happens in our life either physical or Psychological.

The Supreme Spirit (Paramatma) has assigned some duties to be performed to its particle, i.e. Soul (Jeevatma) while on the body of a human.

But once the soul enters into the human body with mind and senses, and the infant grows up, as mentioned in the previous chapter, its mind involves many good and evil actions, desires, etc. and forgets about the obligatory duty which has to be performed while on the body.

Because of that, the human gets into disappointments,

depression, doubt, confusion, etc.

So actually,

The Talk between Krishna and Arjuna means,

The talk between SUPREME SPIRIT (Paramatma) & SOUL (Jeevatma – Mind & Senses)

We need to make understand our minds because the mind is responsible for every happening to a human.

The Supreme wants us to do some duties through us (soul) for the existence of the universe and generations to continue in nature.

Without a Soul with Mind and Senses, the body of a human is just a "dead body".

So, now onwards, let us see what advice the Supreme Spirit (Krishna) has to deliver to its Soul (Mind and Senses) i.e. Arjuna.

Just imagine, a capable friend is giving his hand to one of his friends to get up from the disappointing situation.

The Motivational Speaker enters into the auditorium and seeing the gloomy faces of disappointed persons (many Arjunas), Krishna asks...

Being a human with immense power within you and being a good warrior, why did you make such a gloomy face? Krishna asks him to get up by removing the mental weakness. (2/2-3)

Krishna pointed out his "Mental Weakness", not about "Lack of Skill". He mentions, "being a good warrior or a good fighter or a good soldier, why did you mentally down". Krishna does not doubt Arjuna's skill but here he is weak by the mind.

We all are going into depression when we are unable to win the mind.

Then Arjuna explains Krishna the reason, why he is down by mind because in the battle he has to face many of his Masters (Gurus) and his relatives.

Gurus and Relatives...

Here those Gurus are not on the positive side (Dharma - Pandava's side). If they were good Gurus, they must make understand Dhritarashtra, Duryodhana, etc. (Adharma - Kaurava's side). So according to Krishna, those who are favoring negativity (adharma) must be cleaned.

This 2nd chapter is in three parts :

First from Verses 1 to 39 - Self Realisation

Second from Verses 40 to 53 - Filtration of Duties and Actions

Third from Verses 54 to 72 – Behaviour of Self-Realised Persons.

Dr. Jagadeesh Pillai
PhD in Vedic Science
Four Times Guinness World Record Holder
Winner of MahatmaGandhi Global Peace Award
Author of Many Books

About The Author

Dr. Jagadeesh Pillai a voracious reader, Four Times Guinness World Record holder, writer, and true research scholar was born in Varanasi, the abode of Lord Shiva. He is Ph.D. in Vedic Science. He is a multi-faceted polymath with innate qualities, creative ideas and many remarkable achievements. Although his roots extend back to "Gods own Country"(Kerala), the residents of Varanasi feel proud of him and adore him as a child of Varanasi who caters to every individual in need without any expectations. A deep study into his profile reflects that he has added so many feathers to his cap which makes him quite unique. He is a four times Guinness Book of World Records Holder in the following subjects :

"Script to Screen" which he achieved by producing and directing a state of art animation film within the shortest time possible by breaking the earlier set record by Canadians. There are many national and international Awards and Recognitions to his credit.

Longest Line of Post Cards which he has done on the occasion of 163 years of Indian Postal Day by 16300 post cards. The event was also connected with a questionnaire about Indian Flag.

Largest Poster Awareness Campaign – This was achieved by designing an awareness campaign on the subject "Beti Bachao – Beti Padhao".

Largest Envelop – Towards tribute to Prime Minister's

initiative 'Make in India' – he has created about 4000 sq meter envelop using waste papers.

Attempted by lighting 70000 candles on a 210 kg cake to celebrate the 70th Indian Independence day recorded in World Records India.

Attempted a documentary on Dhamek Stupa of Sarnath dubbing in 17 languages, result is waiting from Guinness World Records.

He is versatile in Gita teaching. The young generation is fond of his Gita teaching and he has changed the life of many young through his continued motivational boost up and teachings.

He has composed and sung Gayatri Mantra in 1000 different tunes.

He has composed and sung Hanuman Chalisa in 108 different tunes.

He has composed and sung hundreds of Sanskrit Bhajans, Patriotic songs, etc.

He has written and directed so many short films and documentaries for awareness campaigns.

He has done voluntary services to UP Police and Kerala Police to spread awareness campaigns on the various issue through videos and photography.

He is on the path of authoring thousands of books on Indian culture, Indian Temples, and the life of extraordinary people.

It is hard to believe that he has produced and directed more than 100 Documentaries on a particular city (Varanasi) which is done by a single person.

He has helped and guided more than 25 boys and girls to achieve world records through various creative and innovative methods.

A multifaceted person who can apply the best of his intellect using the God-given blessings which have been showered upon every human being granting them an immense capacity to learn, experience, and experiment with many things and do wonders in this world of discrimination and disparities.

He is a teacher and a student at the same time who always learns every day and teaches every day. As a master, his weakness was that he never sticks to a particular subject. Perhaps this weakness gives him the strength to master any area which he came across.

Each of his days dawned with learning a new topic and he spend most of his time experimenting and researching it.

He is also a selfless social activist and a motivational speaker.

His life was full of struggle, ups and downs, and failures. But he never gave up and faced all his trials and tribulations full of confidence. Today he is a successful young man with a lot of enthusiasm and rich life experience.

He has sung full Ram Charita Manas 51 hours audio by his own composition. He has also sung the whole Bhagavad-Gita in his own composition with a rhythmic background.

He has also sung "Lokah Samastha Sukhino Bhavantu" in 50 different languages.

Currently working on a detailed and scientific study on Veda, Upanishad, Puranas, Bhagavad Gita, etc.

Currently, he is the Hon' Chancellor of 'Eurasia Digital University'.

Awards

Four Times Guinness World Records

Winner of Mahatma Gandhi Vishwa Shanti Puraskar

Mahatma Gandhi Global Peace Ambassador
Kashi Ratna Award

Dr. APJ Abdul Kalam Motivational Person of the Year 2017

Mother Teresa Award

Indira Gandhi Priyadarshini Award

Bharat Vikas Ratna Award

Udyog Ratna Award

Vigyan Prasar Award

Poorvanchal Ratn Samman

THE SOUL AND ITS TRUE NATURE (Part – 1)

First from Verses 1 to 39 - Self Realisation

So Krishna is starting to teach and make understand his child who is dirtied. As one of our good looking, beautiful children goes for playing with his friends in a good dress on the ground and immediately it starts raining and the ground is filled with water and mud. But the boys are still playing in the rainwater and the ground with mud. The whole body and their dresses completely dirtied. The parents are unable to identify (realize) their kid because all of them are filled with mud from top to bottom.

Parents come close to them, identifies, bring them home and start cleaning them with fresh water, soap, etc.

After a thorough cleaning, the kids clean up, all dirt is washed out and the dresses are removed.

Now again the kid looks beautiful (shining) as earlier (realized and illuminated stage).

While reading this book, you will automatically understand why I give the word "realized" in brackets in some places.

As we know, there are 100s of Children to Dhritarashtra and Gandhaari. Let's consider all of them like negative thoughts, negative actions, desires, attachments that are conquered and dirtied our mind like mud.

Just for example,

Suppose there are 100s of boxes in your mind and each box is filled with a light of ultimate intelligence, wisdom, ideas, and knowledge. Each box has an iron lock and all the locks are rusted. One or few locks are opened and because of that light you are living and understanding the life little bit but still with a lot of confusion, doubts, and disappointments. But, if you can open the other locks one by one, you will become a highly successful person with a lot of good qualities, achievements with more and more good results for yourself and the society.

So let us understand the theme of killing the Children of Gandhaari, as cleaning the dirt locks of the boxes of our mind so that we get a completely cleaned mind removing all confusions and disappointments and light of the wisdom shine self and others.

So, for cleaning a lock, sometimes we can easily clean a lock and open it, sometimes, we need to put oil, etc. to clean the lock, sometimes we need to give pressure on the lock and at some occasions, if the rust is so high, maybe, we need to break the lock by a hammer.

The hardness of the rust in each lock depends on the pressure and force needed to open the lock.

Many life situations, which are making your mind down and making you disappoint are the rust in the lock and you are unknown the way to overcome it.

Good quality of life with high intelligence depends on how many boxes of your mind are opened.

There are many multi-talented personalities around the world, who has done many inspiring things in their life irrespective of miserable life situations. They never sit with disappointments and complaints, when one or two locks of the boxes of their mind was rusted and was unlocking it. They kept trying and one by one, they unlocked it using different methods. By unlocking one by one, you can increase the light of intelligence, wisdom, ideas, and knowledge.

The same cleaning process is going to happen now onwards.

When the Supreme Spirit (Krishna - Paramatma) sent the Soul (Jeevatma - Arjuna), it was clean like Krishna, but when it entered into the body and when the kids grew up, it gets dirtied with necessary and unnecessary thoughts, desires, interests, ethical and non-ethical actions, doubts, confusions, etc. and he forgets and confuses about the exact duties to be performed in life.

There is a saying that we get the birth as human after going through many births as other creatures like birds, animals, etc. and in front of us, the human is indeed the most excellent creation on earth. If we look into the world, the power of the human is limitless and we human can only read, write, understand, experience, innovate, discover and experiment. We cannot speak in a language with any other creature in the universe and make them understand and they reply in any language. Since our understanding level is high, Krishna can easily explain the wisdom and we can understand it easily.

So here, the wisdom, which Krishna is delivering to Arjuna, is of some cleaning elements to clean the mind.

It is not good for a human with unlimited capacities and capabilities to down the mind with unnecessary desires, attachments, doubts, and confusion. Once we know it, we should immediately throw away those things from our minds, which makes us pain, agony, disappointment, etc. There are thousands of situations (of many kinds) in life will come which will disturb our mind and it will reflect in our life.

If you are disappointed, it does not mean that something wrong happened to you. There are many reasons for disappointment. For example, you had a wish to get something and for which you are not qualified, even after many attempts, you are not getting the expecting result. This will make you unhappy and if one of your friends achieves it, it will make you disappoint the mind.

So here, you are pained with a situation aroused because of not meeting the reality as with what you were expecting.

Now just see, is there anybody responsible for your disappointment? No. But when our expectation doesn't meet with reality, it is our habit to blame others. Nobody has forced you to accept the pain. Nobody has forced you to bring up the ego within you when one of your friends achieves a competition.

We are only responsible. We have many options. Either we try our best more than earlier to achieve it or choose other options. When somebody achieves, praise them, motivate them, instead we do the opposite of praise and motivate because of jealousy.

So, in the above example, there were two things, desire and jealous which have pained our mind. Both of these attitudes are negative.

An Important Quote to understand....

Whatever happens to us, there is a reason behind it. For every effect, there is a cause. Not all bad situations happen to us, because of others. In most of the cases, we are only responsible. We wish that people behave or react, the way we want. It's not possible. All of them are forced to perform duties per the quality of their mind and senses. We are the master of our mind, not of others. If we try to intervene and force to manage the mind of others, with our thoughts, intentions, and desires, we will disturb our minds and others too.

"Problems.." most of the people are facing one or other problems. But there is a left and right part of every problem.

Left Side - Many reasons behind it for the problem we are facing.

Right Side - Multiple Options to overcome it.

But, what we normally do. We always concentrate on the LEFT side, problems, problems, problems and we blame others for our problems and also make others responsible for it. As I mentioned earlier, if there is an effect, there is a cause and this cause maybe some bad karmas from our previous birth or past life and according to science "Every action there is an equal and opposite reaction".

But nobody wants to blame themselves and finding it easy to blame others.

But if we go through the RIGHT side, there are multiple options to overcome it.

So the book of Bhagavad Gita contents multiple options to overcome any kind of negative situation in life.

Let me recall the quote of Swami Vivekananda from Kathopanishad (Verse-14).

UDHISHTATA JAAGRADA PRAPYA VARANNIBODHAT,

KSHURASYA DHARA NISHITA DURATYAYA DURGAM

PATASTAT KAVAYOVADANTI

(Arise, Awake and Stop not till the Goal is achieved and it is not that easy to achieve because you have to face many difficult situations in life, many arrows from others to chase).

The confused Arjuna (disappointed mind and senses, a disciple of Krishna), submitting Krishna (his Master, Boss, Creator), and pleading him to clean his confusions, doubts, and disappointments and requesting him to advise the proper methods to overcome from it. By all means, he is getting ready to like an obedient disciple and he forces Krishna to deliver the teachings. A disciple must be eager and dedicated to getting the teachings of a teacher. (Gita 2/7),

Here onwards, Krishna (The Supreme Spirit) starts his teachings to his disciple Arjuna (Soul with Mind and Senses).

As mentioned earlier, we humans are highly intelligent people. But, at the same time, we weep for not getting something which is unethical. Our strong desire, love, and attachment with something create pain when we have to lose it. Here we are not using our intelligence to ascertain the quality of the relations. We are in blind love and attachment with something of evil nature. Krishna says, use your intelligence, and don't keep on losing those habits, attitudes within you which are evil. (2/11)

Krishna (The Supreme Spirit, the Creator) always exists and Arjuna (The Soul with Mind and Senses) being a part and particle of Krishna will also exit always. Only the carrier of the Soul, means, the body will damage and lose because the body is perishable as the life cycle of the body from infant to old age completes, the body will perish and the Soul will take a new body to continue its duties, developments, and responsibilities to be performed per the order of The Supreme Spirit (Krishna).

Once we understand the difference of what exactly we are going to lose, such people never worry. Is the Soul is Important or the Body is important?. (2/12-13)

Whatever we experience through our body, are the effect in the mind and senses. The effect on the mind will change like we are happy on some occasions and we are unhappy on some occasions. We were very happy when we were enjoying with friends in college days and we were very unhappy when the college days complete and on farewell. The whole college days passed happily but the missing of our close friends made an effect on our mind because of losing them. But this unhappiness is not going to be there for permanent. It will gradually change. Such situations of sometimes happiness and sometime un-happiness will come and go like climate changes. Those who understand it never weeps. He knows that the situation is temporary. (2/13-15).

We had nothing so we lost nothing. For example, happiness and un-happiness – both are not two different situations and not an always existing one, rather the situation of happiness aroused when the effect of an incident to our mind was of pleasure nature and un-happiness aroused when the effect of an incident to our mind was opposite to it.

Happiness and Un-happiness have not existed, both generated in a situation and the effect on the mind differentiates it.

For a more clear understanding of it. Just imagine, do we always cry or laugh? No. we remain calm and normal. We react when something happens in any situation. For example, while reading a book, you were looking quiet and calm, not happy and un-happy, just normal. But immediately there is a call on your mobile and when you pick up, the person of the other end informs you that you are passed on your last attempt at IAS. Now imagine the situation. (2/16).

Now onwards, (2/17 to 2/39), Krishna (The Supreme Spirit) explains Arjuna (The Soul with Mind and Senses), about the reality and quality of the Soul.

Let's recall what we mentioned earlier, about the soul entry into the mother's womb for a new child. There are many methods to see whether the body of the child is formed or not, inside the mother's womb. Till the entry of the soul, the body is just like one of the parts of the organ for the mother. But once the soul enters into it, the body starts movements. When the movements of the body start, then only we consider the growth of the child.

Through many methods, we can see the body, but with no methods, we cannot see the Soul.

Since you can see the body, you can damage it, operate it, and you can remove it. But how can you do anything with the Soul, because it's invisible? We cannot do anything with that invisible soul. We and our bodies are alive because of the soul and not the soul alive because of us or our bodies.

Krishna (The Supreme Spirit) is surrounded by the universe like the divinity or the power of the soul is surrounded all over our body, that's why we feel, whenever somebody touches any part of our body. So, it's difficult to destroy or perish the Soul.

Those are ignorant who believe that when the body dies, the soul also dies. The soul never kills anybody and anybody can kill the soul. When the body dies, the soul remains.

Krishna explains to Arjuna, to kill the negativities of mind. For example, if Arjuna has to Kill Duryodhana, as I explained earlier about 100s of boxes in our mind with rusted lock, Duryodhana (one of the sons of Dhritrashtra) is a kind of hard rust on a lock of one of the boxes. Kill Duryodhana means, kill the evil habit of Duryodhana's nature, (cleaning the rust of the lock of one of the boxes).

The process of such cleaning of the mind of the Soul does not happen in one body. The soul with the mind of senses when in one body, it dirts (rust) whenever the mind involves in a negative action of evil nature. When the mind realizes the fault and changes the nature from evil to goodness, it will clean. Sometimes the clean remains permanent and sometimes, it rusts again when the mind involves in any evil action. So the process of unlocking the locks of boxes one by one is going one. The unlocking process of the rusted locks of the mind is a continuous process and it won't happen to be in one body. The capacity of the body to handle the Soul with mind and senses, for further development diminishes, the Soul will leave the body like we change clothes and will take a new body. We can assume that the Soul also needs a different location and different situation to experience the further cleaning process of the mind and senses in it.

Suppose, we have 100 boxes with 100 locks (One Soul with mind and senses). All are rusted and unable to unlock it. Somebody asked us (the Soul) to go to Karnataka (Body), an expert (positivities) there can unlock few locks. So we (the Soul) landed in Karnataka and met the rust cleaner of the lock. He asked us (the Soul) to stay there for some time to clean and unlock it. He accommodated us (the Soul) and stayed for 2 months. He, the expert (positivities) tried many methods (goodness's) but was able to open only one lock.

He, the expert asked us to leave the place Karnataka (our body) and go to another expert of Kashmir (another body), the expert there (more good deeds and actions) can unlock more locks.

So you (the Soul) leaves Karnataka (your Body) and flies to Kashmir (your new body) and meets the new expert, and the new expert accommodates you for few months and tries to clean the rust of the lock of some other boxes by using more cleaning solutions (more good actions and deeds), and he can clean and unlock only one lock of one box of the mind and then the Soul has to leave Kashmir (the body), and for more cleaning and unlocking of the lock, it has to go to another state (another body) and meet other experts (more good action and deeds).

Since the cleaning process of mind of the Soul is going on and to complete the process, the Soul has to meet many experts (experience and practice of many good deeds and actions), the Soul will change bodies and the mind cleaning process will continue until the lock of the last box is opened. When the last lock of the box unlocks, the process of unlocking all the boxes completes, means, the Soul purification process is completed and the lights of intelligence and wisdom start illuminating. When the complete mind purification happens, the Soul matches with the quality of the Supreme (Krishna). Since the purification, the process of the mind of the Soul is completed and the Soul's quality with purified mind matches with the Supreme, the Soul needs not to take any more bodies and joins with the Supreme Spirit.

We can see many people in our surroundings with some kind of divine qualities who are always engaged in selfless services, teaching, helping, no bondage with anybody or anything, no interest in accumulating wealth or any kind of physical things, etc., it means through many births the mind of his Soul was in the process of cleaning and very soon in this birth or next birth or so, his soul will complete the process of cleaning and will join with the Supreme.

We can also understand the mind purification of the Soul method as we enter into the school from LKG and after attending many levels of class we reach Ph.D. and D.Litt. Our intelligence, wisdom and understanding level when at LKG was different and now after completing D.Litt is different.

The same change we can experience from the people around us.

Pessimist (in Lower Classes) - Ignorant, egoist, criminals, over pride, over smart, always angry, find wrong in everything, always doubtful, alcoholic, self-praising, over-attachment with family members, discrimination, etc.

Optimists (in Higher Classes) - Down to earth, good attitude, cool, mercy, always forgiving, helping nature, teaching, innovating, creating, multi-talents, etc.

Above, I have mentioned Soul as "Soul with Mind and Senses". Since the Soul is an extension or part and particle of Supreme, no purification is required to the Soul. But the actual purification is required to the mind and senses which are connected with the Soul.

For example, a Coconut is a part of Coconut Tree (Supreme), looks perfect from outside, but when we break it, the white fruit (Mind and Senses) is not good, either damaged, perished or tasteless. But, no change or nothing happened to the hard outer surface of that coconut (Soul). Even before break it, we never assumed that the white fruit part inside would be of bad quality. (Verse 2/25)

Those who born will die in one day, nobody can stop it. Even if one lives for 100 years, it will be for 36,500 days. We know that one in a hundred thousand people may live up to 100 years, which means any day or any year before 100 years, we must leave this world.

An important quote to note.....

According to the present scenario, we have approx.70 years of healthy life means 26500 days. If we deduct childhood and sleeping time, we have only around 10,000 days to live on our stand on this earth. Last century this day, we were not here, next century this day we will not be here. Past life is not clear to us, next life is also not clear to us. It's a truth and fact, then worrying has no sense. (2/27-28).

So, forget about those issues (related to the body, soul, etc.) which are beyond the control of a human, since those are associated with fixed truth and fact of life.

What we have to concentrate on and understand is our birth as a human, and the duties to be performed. Being human, we have been blessed with immense qualities and intelligence and we have to use those capabilities to excel in our duties. We must feel lucky that we got birth as a human for which we might have taken many other births in the past and might have done many good karmas and experience.

Each creature on this earth is embedded with some duties to be performed and the of all is different. What the bird will do, an animal cannot do and vice-versa. Even in humans also, nature, qualifications, and qualities are different. Each one of them will perform their actions per the dominancy of quality and nature embedded within them.

Suppose there is a Doctor. He may be a good doctor or a bad doctor. The doctor performs his action as a doctor. How good he is in his profession, depends on his intention, quality of thoughts, selfless service, etc. Same as in many other professions.

But we must concentrate and try to do better and better in our attitude, habits, and actions. Intervening on other's actions is not our duty. They are responsible for their actions. We are responsible for our actions. We should try our best to improve ourselves. If you strongly feel dislikes somebody's action, you don't apply it to you. But if you are going to dislike his actions, protest, try to change him, you will be in trouble. But most of the people misbalances their mind and carries pain in mind, thinking of somebody else's action. Nothing going to be permanent here, whatever attachment you have with anything or anybody here on the earth, one day it will break and taken back away from you forever.

Just concentrate on you and check whether you performed your part better or not.

Suppose there is a colleague in your office, he is always buttering the boss of the company, not performing his duties properly and even after this, his days are perfectly going on. You dis-likes his attitude and actions because you have to properly do your duties and to hard work to get the salary and still there is no appreciation from the boss.

This issue will disturb your mind and you will start abuse and condemn him by the mind and will share your feeling with others. Your mind became jealous and you are very disturbed. You lost your concentration in your job and your excellence diminishes.

The other staff did nothing wrong to you, he never comes to you, never abused you, he was just performing his actions. Buttering the boss, time pass, not doing the duties properly, etc. were his actions. Now itself, he is perfect, but you are disturbed.

Instead of giving better performance in your duty and actions, you tried to check and verify the action of others. Jealous developed in your mind, the desire of appreciation from boss generated in your mind and to satisfy your mind, you started abusing him, condemn him and trying to hurt him. You want to win him by defaming him.

You think that you are better and the other is wrong. Just think over your actions, which caused you to disturb your mind and then decide who is good and who is wrong.

You were wrong. Your duty was just to concentrate on your job and actions and improve you better and better day by day and satisfy with it.

The other person did nothing. He was just silent. He was just performing his duties. Who told you to intervene in his actions, to check and verify it.

You un-necessarily invited things in your mind and disturbed it by intervening on other's duties and actions.

That way you have generated so many bad karmas. He never abused you, but you did. He never condemns you, but you did, he never defames you, but you did.

Whatever way he was performing his duties and activities in the office, he never disturbed you and so never generated any bad karma. But you were perfect in your duties and actions in the office, but still, you generated a lot of bad karma just because of intervening in his duties. (2/31-32).

So, here, when such conflicts and disturbs arise in mind, try to win your mind, otherwise, you will be in trouble. It will be a shame for a human, who by jealousy, greedy and anger on others disturbs his mind and are depressed. You should realize that I did bad karma and need to fight with your mind to clear the dirt and to get up from disappointments (2/33).

Because of jealousy and greed, you had abused and condemn the other person and have exchanged wrong about him in the public to defame him. But when the public understands later that you were the actual culprit, and you made false allegations about your colleague under the influence of jealous and greed developed in your mind, all those people you had praised you earlier, will start hating you and will be treated as a looser which will make you more regretful in the future. People will start discussing stories about your mental disabilities. (2/ 34-36).

An important quote to note :

When I was explaining the above story in a class, a student asked me about the reaction of the other staff who was innocent but had to face the action of that jealous staff. What he would have done, when the jealous person abused him, condemn him and tried to defame him in public and why he had to face it.

Every effect there is a cause. Then, what would be the cause?

1) From his boss buttering attitude, we can understand that he is lazy and selfish and he might be doing such many un-ethical actions in life. Either someway, he has to face it.

2) How it affected him.

If he is intelligent and understands that, the other person is blaming me because of jealousy of my connection and freedom with the boss. He can either react or bypass. If he has taken the issue in his mind, then he will be pained and react. Otherwise, he will keep silent and forgive him without reacting and doing anything against the jealous colleague.

If he reacts, oppose and anger (again generates more bad karma). If he forgets and forgives (no more bad karma generates, instead some of his old bad karma's can be removed).

3) If the jealous person later understands that he did bad karma of abusing him by jealous and ask for forgiveness to his friend and his friend wholeheartedly forgives (the bad karma generated by him will diminish)

Our minds should not disturb and not take any action because we dislike other's actions and attitudes. If we have, a habit of disliking people and reacting to it based on people's actions and attitudes, we are generating bad karma. Apart from that we will accept and reject people.

But once we understand the theory of guna dominancy in each one's action. We will only reject the guna, not the person.

A developed mind means, immense happiness, open to all irrespective of caste, creed, action, attitude, character, etc.

We are developed, they are underdeveloped – that's all !!! We can see many people in our society who are lazy to do something. Some have fear to do something. Before trying anything in life, they will sit back thinking about its result. Before trying anything, they will accept failure. But, we should try and fight back with every hurdle in life, we should not think about the win and failure, gain and lose, etc., if we won we can enjoy the result, even if we fail, we can learn and experience many things. At least we can say, we tried. Nobody will blame us that we didn't try for it.

Up to this, Krishna explained to us to realize self (Soul), its connections, qualities, and the differentiation of soul and body. (2/37-39).

THE SOUL AND ITS TRUE NATURE (Part - 2)

Second from Verses 40 to 53

Filtration of Duties and Actions

Considering our duty, whatever action we do in our life without the fear of loss or any other issues, even if we have to stop in between, it never goes waste. Even the little bit of experience we gained will remain in our soul and some way it will help in the future. Apart from that, it will also help us to unlock some rusted locks of the boxes in our minds. (2/40).

Only those who understand the self (soul) and dedicated to doing every action by concentrating and understanding the reality of the Supreme Spirit and Soul can only reach the real destination of life and enjoy the fruit of life. (2/41).

Those are fools, who are involved in finding shortcuts and other ways to achieve heaven and believing in heavenly achievement whenever they fulfill their desires. They forget about their real duties and commitments towards our society and other fellow humans.

Their actions depend on the dominancy of any one of the three Gunas (qualities) which are called Satwik (Daivik), Rajasik (Manushya) and Thamasik (Asuriya).

Sattwa Guna – Virtue and Purity in every action, mostly selfless.

Rajasik – Attraction, attachment, liking, and longing, selfish.

Tamasik – Binds by negligence, indolence, and sleep.

Knowledge, wisdom, and understanding about self and the actions to be performed are always useful throughout life and in the next incarnation too. (2/46)

We should do the actions (karma) without expecting it's fruit. We have no authority to decide the fruit for your actions and no specific expectations must be there in mind to experience the fruit of actions. All actions must be done with a selfless mind. We also should not sit idle without doing any karmas (actions). Practicing selfless actions are also like cleaning of a rusted lock. So fearlessly, without expectations, we must do our actions. Practice and achieving the balancing of the mind is called Yoga (mental balancing achievement) (2/47-48).

Any action with mental balancing (without the tension of its fruit) will be considered as divine karma (an action of higher quality) and selfless Action. Sometime, they may be physical gains nothing for their actions, but they might have generated a lot of good karmas by their selfless mentality and actions. But those who do every action or karma expecting its fruit will be selfish and will face many happy and un-happy situations throughout life (2/49).

Those who have achieved the Yoga state (achievement of mental balancing), will sacrifice (forget) the past good and bad experiences in this birth itself.

Forgetting means, they won't carry any tension in the mind. Keeping the tension in mind will disturb and it will be rusting one of the locks of the boxes of mind. So we should practice achieving mental balancing, through continuous effort and practice we can achieve it (2/50).

Such people who have achieved the 'state of mental balancing', detach them from any fruits of actions and also detach them from any kind of physical attachment (body) and mental attachment (soul). They easily unlock all the locks of the boxes of mind and achieves illumination and connects with the Supreme (2/51).

Once we overcome the ignorance and understand the difference between the soul and body, we will be able to analyze whatever situations come in our way in our life and will be able to take proper actions intelligently, without any tensions and confusions (2/52).

When our consciousness, understanding, and intelligence
constantly connect and dedicate to Supreme while doing
any action, we will achieve self-realization and mental
balancing (2/53).

THE SOUL AND ITS TRUE NATURE (Part - 3)

Third from Verses 54 to 72 – Behaviour of Self-Realised Persons

Here, Arjuna asks Krishna to explain the qualities and behavior of Self-Realised persons who have achieved the state of Mental Balancing. How they speak, how they sit, how they walk, how they react etc. (2/54)

Those who sacrifice all desires of the mind, remove all tensions and anger, removes ego, removes mental bondage and attachments, no fight with anybody, no jealous, maintain a clear mind, bans any kind of un-necessary thoughts, finding self in everything, mental satisfaction through selfless action, etc.

No fear, silent, who understands everything is part of Supreme (Brahman), seeing the self in everything.

Those self-realized people will never attempt to dig good and bad in others and will behave accordingly.

He disconnects the senses (draw them back) from all those evil things, which may dirt and disturbs his mind as the tortoise draws in his limbs into the shell.

He intelligently manages every action and situation and by trying not to disturb the mind. Once the mind is disturbed, it will lead to creating any type of unnecessary problems, including distress, disappointments, etc. (2/ 55-58).

Controlling the senses is not that easy. We can try to withdraw our senses from desires, but the desire to achieve pleasure will remain. But, once we realize and understand the reality of Supreme and Soul, the desire will also gradually remove from the mind. Suppose, if there is an alcoholic who has stopped his habit of taking liquor by the pressure of somebody, but his desire to take it will remain in his mind. He stopped it by extreme pressure on him because of his health issues. But he never realized the consequences and stopped it by himself. There is a big difference in stopping a habit by the force of somebody and by himself by self-realization. The desire will remain if stopped by somebody's force (if he sees that somebody taking alcohol, his interest to take it will arise in his mind, because the desire and enjoyment of it are still alive in his mind) but if stopped by himself without anybody's pressure means, his desire also killed in his mind and so he stopped the habit.

The same thing we can understand differently – suppose there is an alcoholic and he has some wound in his mouth and difficult to eat and drink. So he stopped taking alcohol. We cannot say that he killed his desire or habit of taking it in his mind. Just temporarily stopped by force, as soon as his mouth is perfect and health, he will start again. (2/59).

It will be very difficult for the mind of even wise scholars/sages who have already achieved a higher degree of self-control to control the senses. The un-killed, hidden or sleeping desire will sometime wakeup and disturb his spiritual development process and practices. To further achieve a higher degree of complete self-realization and to kill any kind of desire in mind, a lot of selfless karma (action) has to be practiced. Mostly the desire in mind awakes when the action involves any kind of selfishness. Selfless means, whatever Karma I do for anybody must be dedicated to the Supreme without any kind of expectation. Even we did something for a person, we should think that we did it for the Soul of a person and the Soul of a person is connected with Supreme. Expectation arises when we do something for human beings to imagine him as a physical being with a body.

The intelligent spiritual development happens when we do something for the Soul which is connected with Supreme. Such actions will remain permanent. Suppose, if we helped a person with some money in an emergency and before returning it, he dies. For us, the amount we helped also lost. Yes, if we did help him thinking that we helped a body, then we lost it. But if our intention while helping was that we are helping a Soul, then the help provided remains forever and either way it will come back to you also. Of course, it may not be money or through the same person.

Whatever action one do, if his/her intelligence, intention, etc. are constantly connected and dedicated with Supreme, then we can say that his/her Karma is selfless with a balanced mind, self-realized and self-centered.

The way of actions and activities of a self-realized person will be different than others. He won't search for God outside, rather he feels him in God and whatever he does will be in compliment to God and for the benefit of others. Selfish thoughts like "me, mine" will be merged with the Supreme.

An important quote to note :

If we helped a person (person with a physical body) – we expect help in return from him, and when we require help, we will approach him for a return help and mostly he will refuse. He may or may not be in a position to help, but he refused to help us back. At that time, we will get angry with that person and may develop many hot issues between him and us. When he dies, your expectation to get back it from him also dies, but the thought of it will remain.

But at the same time, if we helped somebody thinking that we are helping a soul in a body because the soul is never perishable and connected to supreme. Then, when we are in need, we won't ask that person to help back. Even if we ask and he refuses, we won't get pained. We will directly pray to the Supreme with full faith and with a calm mind and we will confidently face the situation. Later we will see that the issue of us for which we seek help has been solved either by ourselves or through any other person. Even if that person whom we helped dies, our intention, thought and the selfless action remains in the universe through the "Soul to Supreme" forever and either way in the future it will come back to us.

Selfless Karma is like a Saving Bank account of Good Karmas earned by good deeds with good intentions towards our service and dedication to Supreme. Even if we die, it will remain.

Selfish Karma is like temporary earnings to fulfill physical desires which will easily spend on necessary and unnecessary things and when we die, only bad deeds, bad intentions, etc. will remain as our meaningless earnings.

If we are leaving an uncontrolled mind and it senses to wander here and there to find different kind of pleasures by desires, and when we are unable to fulfill those desires, anger will develop, and when we are angry, we will take un-wise decisions and our memory will also disturb. Gradually, our consciousness and intelligence will down and from there onwards, all our further decisions and activities in life will affect. We can see many persons and families who spoil their life, just because they were unable to properly use their intelligence and wise decisions to manage the adverse situation in life.

We can see many persons in our surroundings; they take quick actions in extreme anger when something happens without thinking about the consequences later. But if the same person immediately balances the situation by the mind without shouting and taking any quick action, he can manage the situation with a good result without disturbing him or anything. For that, he has to sit quietly and to control the mind and senses cool and calm. When in a cool mind, his good intelligence activates and can make wise decisions (2/63-65).

Those who are not in a position to control the mind and senses are even unaware of the existence of soul and supreme. Because of that unawareness, they will continuously involve in such activities by the mind and senses by desires. They will always be disturbed without peace and harmony in any field of his life (2/66).

Like the boat in the ocean moves in improper directions in heavy wind and storm, and uncontrollable to manage in a specific direction by the boatman, the mind also improperly moves the intelligence from a stable state of it. Hence, wise decisions and specific directions are not possible. When intelligence is in a stable state of mind, we can make wise decisions, generate good ideas, develop creations, innovations, etc.

<u>*An important quote to note :*</u>

We can see many extraordinary plus persons, multi-talented people, multi-achievers, constant research personals, voracious readers, etc. They are also living in the same society with the same surroundings and situations. But how those people became highly intelligent, not all people of society. There is no magic and they are not special. The only difference is that they understood the quality of a stable state of mind and to accomplish it, they do not involve un-necessary things which disturb or tension their mind. They never become jealous, they never get angry with anybody, they never compete, anybody, they never involve in such things which waste time, money and disturb the mind.

They will always involve in such things, which make them cool by the mind, and when the mind is cool, dirt free and stable; their intelligence will be in a highly developed stage. When the intelligence and consciousness are highly developed and the mind is stable, we can do en-number good things, creations, innovations, discoveries, etc. We can develop from a common person to an uncommon or highly developed being.

There are many such personalities in our society like Dr. APJ Abdul Kalam, Sachin Tendulkar, etc. and usually we call them "down-to-earth" people. We can think that somebody throws a stone to them on their face direction and they immediately face down not to touch the stone on their face. The stone here represents for abuses, jealous of others, unnecessary desires, time-wasting activities, etc.

I recall a quote seen in a hospital that "The successful person built the house of his success by the stones others thrown to him). (2/67-68)

The consciousness of mentally highly developed intelligent people is like they are always awake even in sleep. It doesn't mean that they are sleeping with open eyes at night. Awake means, they will be intelligently balancing and managing any kind of adverse situation and human relationships.

People who have no control over mind and the senses are always wandering here and there to fulfill their desires with an unsatisfactory mind and because of that they lose their intelligence and proper consciousness means, they turn in sleeping mode.

Developed intelligence means we have a torchlight with loaded battery, which immediately illuminates when there is dark. But if the intelligence and consciousness are down it will work like a torchlight with poor battery power and it doesn't work properly when needed. (2/69).

Just think about the ocean with immense water in it and still it constantly stable within and not disturbs, overflows, or reacts because of joining many rivers on it. Just imagine that thousands of rivers join the ocean every day from every corner, but when we see the ocean, it looks quite, calm and stable. This is one more example to maintain a peaceful mind whatever adverse situation comes around you. (2/70)

Those who with constant practice and understanding, give ups all un-necessary desires, feeling of jealousy, selfishness, ego, competition with others, me-mine attitude, etc., will experience ultimate peace of mind. (2/71).

Whenever, one constantly practices self-realization, understanding Soul and Supreme, control over the mind, senses, and desires, concentration over words and deeds, maintaining a balanced mind on any situations around you – will achieve high-level spiritual development, will develop higher intelligence to perform great things in life and will enjoy permanent peace of mind (2/72).

English text of slokhas of 2nd Chapter are available in this book for quick reference.

Slokas of Bhagavad Gita Chapter-2 in English Text form for Quick Reference

1

sañjaya uvācha

taṁ tathā kṛipayāviṣhṭamaśhru pūrṇākulekṣhaṇam

viṣhīdantamidaṁ vākyam

2

śhrī bhagavān uvācha
kutastvā kaśhmalamidaṁ viṣhame samupasthitam
anārya-juṣhṭamaswargyam akīrti-karam arjuna

3

klaibyaṁ mā sma gamaḥ pārtha naitat tvayyupapadyate
kṣhudraṁ hṛidaya-daurbalyaṁ tyaktvottiṣhṭha parantapa

4

arjuna uvācha
kathaṁ bhīṣhmam ahaṁ sankhye droṇaṁ cha madhusūdana
iṣhubhiḥ pratiyotsyāmi pūjārhāvari-sūdana

5

gurūnahatvā hi mahānubhāvān
śhreyo bhoktuṁ bhaikṣhyamapīha loke
hatvārtha-kāmāṁstu gurūnihaiva
bhuñjīya bhogān rudhira-pradigdhān

6

na chaitadvidmaḥ kataranno garīyo
yadvā jayema yadi vā no jayeyuḥ
yāneva hatvā na jijīviṣhāmas
te 'vasthitāḥ pramukhe dhārtarāṣhṭrāḥ

7

kārpaṇya-doṣhopahata-svabhāvaḥ
pṛichchhāmi tvāṁ dharma-sammūḍha-chetāḥ
yach-chhreyaḥ syānniśhchitaṁ brūhi tanme
śhiṣhyaste 'haṁ śhādhi māṁ tvāṁ prapannam

8

na hi prapaśhyāmi mamāpanudyād
yach-chhokam uchchhoṣhaṇam-indriyāṇām
avāpya bhūmāv-asapatnamṛiddhaṁ
rājyaṁ surāṇāmapi chādhipatyam

9

sañjaya uvācha
evam-uktvā hṛiṣhīkeśhaṁ guḍākeśhaḥ parantapa

na yotsya iti govindam uktvā tūṣhṇīṁ babhūva ha

10

tam-uvācha hṛiṣhīkeśhaḥ prahasanniva bhārata
senayorubhayor-madhye viṣhīdantam-idaṁ vachaḥ

11

śhrī bhagavān uvācha
aśhochyān-anvaśhochas-tvaṁ prajñā-vādānśh cha bhāṣhase
gatāsūn-agatāsūnśh-cha nānuśhochanti paṇḍitāḥ

12

na tvevāhaṁ jātu nāsaṁ na tvaṁ neme janādhipāḥ
na chaiva na bhaviṣhyāmaḥ sarve vayamataḥ param

13

dehino 'smin yathā dehe kaumāraṁ yauvanaṁ jarā
tathā dehāntara-prāptir dhīras tatra na muhyati

14

mātrā-sparśhās tu kaunteya śhītoṣhṇa-sukha-duḥkha-dāḥ
āgamāpāyino 'nityās tans-titikṣhasva bhārata

15

yaṁ hi na vyathayantyete puruṣhaṁ puruṣharṣhabha
sama-duḥkha-sukhaṁ dhīraṁ so 'mṛitatvāya kalpate

16

*nāsato vidyate bhāvo nābhāvo vidyate sataḥ
ubhayorapi dṛiṣhṭo 'nta stvanayos tattva-darśhibhiḥ*

17

*avināśhi tu tadviddhi yena sarvam idaṁ tatam
vināśham avyayasyāsya na kaśhchit kartum arhati*

18

*antavanta ime dehā nityasyoktāḥ śharīriṇaḥ
anāśhino 'prameyasya tasmād yudhyasva bhārata*

19

*ya enaṁ vetti hantāraṁ yaśh chainaṁ manyate hatam
ubhau tau na vijānīto nāyaṁ hanti na hanyate*

20

*na jāyate mriyate vā kadāchin
nāyaṁ bhūtvā bhavitā vā na bhūyaḥ
ajo nityaḥ śhāśhvato 'yaṁ purāṇo
na hanyate hanyamāne śharīre*

21

*vedāvināśhinaṁ nityaṁ ya enam ajam avyayam
kathaṁ sa puruṣhaḥ pārtha kaṁ ghātayati hanti kam*

22

vāsānsi jīrṇāni yathā vihāya
navāni grihṇāti naro 'parāṇi
tathā sharīrāṇi vihāya jīrṇānya
nyāni sanyāti navāni dehī

23

nainaṁ chhindanti shastrāṇi nainaṁ dahati pāvakaḥ
na chainaṁ kledayantyāpo na shoṣhayati mārutaḥ

24

achchhedyo 'yam adāhyo 'yam akledyo 'shoṣhya eva cha
nityaḥ sarva-gataḥ sthāṇur achalo 'yaṁ sanātanaḥ

25

avyakto 'yam achintyo 'yam avikāryo 'yam uchyate
tasmādevaṁ viditvainaṁ nānushochitum arhasi

26

atha chainaṁ nitya-jātaṁ nityaṁ vā manyase mṛitam
tathāpi tvaṁ mahā-bāho naivaṁ shochitum arhasi

27

jātasya hi dhruvo mṛityur dhruvaṁ janma mṛitasya cha
tasmād aparihārye 'rthe na tvaṁ shochitum arhasi

28

avyaktādīni bhūtāni vyakta-madhyāni bhārata
avyakta-nidhanānyeva tatra kā paridevanā

29

āśhcharya-vat paśhyati kaśhchid enan
āśhcharya-vad vadati tathaiva chānyaḥ
āśhcharya-vach chainam anyaḥ śhṛiṇoti
śhrutvāpyenaṁ veda na chaiva kaśhchit

30

dehī nityam avadhyo 'yaṁ dehe sarvasya bhārata
tasmāt sarvāṇi bhūtāni na tvaṁ śhochitum arhasi

31

swa-dharmam api chāvekṣhya na vikampitum arhasi
dharmyāddhi yuddhāch chhreyo 'nyat kṣhatriyasya na vidyate

32

yadṛichchhayā chopapannaṁ swarga-dvāram apāvṛitam
sukhinaḥ kṣhatriyāḥ pārtha labhante yuddham īdṛiśham

33

atha chet tvam imaṁ dharmyaṁ saṅgrāmaṁ na kariṣhyasi
tataḥ sva-dharmaṁ kīrtiṁ cha hitvā pāpam avāpsyasi

34

*akīrtiṁ chāpi bhūtāni
kathayiṣhyanti te 'vyayām
sambhāvitasya chākīrtir
maraṇād atirichyate*

35

*bhayād raṇād uparataṁ mansyante tvāṁ mahā-rathāḥ
yeṣhāṁ cha tvaṁ bahu-mato bhūtvā yāsyasi lāghavam*

36

*avāchya-vādānśh cha bahūn vadiṣhyanti tavāhitāḥ
nindantastava sāmarthyaṁ tato duḥkhataraṁ nu kim*

37

*hato vā prāpsyasi swargaṁ jitvā vā bhokṣhyase mahīm
tasmād uttiṣhṭha kaunteya yuddhāya kṛita-niśhchayaḥ*

38

*sukha-duḥkhe same kṛitvā lābhālābhau jayājayau
tato yuddhāya yujyasva naivaṁ pāpam avāpsyasi*

39

*eṣhā te 'bhihitā sānkhye
buddhir yoge tvimāṁ śhṛiṇu
buddhyā yukto yayā pārtha*

karma-bandhaṁ prahāsyasi

40

nehābhikrama-nāśho 'sti pratyavāyo na vidyate
svalpam apyasya dharmasya trāyate mahato bhayāt

41

vyavasāyātmikā buddhir ekeha kuru-nandana
bahu-śhākhā hyanantāśh cha buddhayo 'vyavasāyinām

42, 43

yāmimāṁ puṣhpitāṁ vāchaṁ pravadanty-avipaśhchitaḥ
veda-vāda-ratāḥ pārtha nānyad astīti vādinaḥ
kāmātmānaḥ swarga-parā janma-karma-phala-pradām
kriyā-viśheṣha-bahulāṁ bhogaiśhwarya-gatiṁ prati

44

bhogaiśwvarya-prasaktānāṁ tayāpahṛita-chetasām
vyavasāyātmikā buddhiḥ samādhau na vidhīyate

45

trai-guṇya-viṣhayā vedā nistrai-guṇyo bhavārjuna
nirdvandvo nitya-sattva-stho niryoga-kṣhema ātmavān

46

yāvān artha udapāne sarvataḥ samplutodake
tāvānsarveṣhu vedeṣhu brāhmaṇasya vijānataḥ

47

karmaṇy-evādhikāras te mā phaleṣhu kadāchana
mā karma-phala-hetur bhūr mā te saṅgo 'stvakarmaṇi

48

yoga-sthaḥ kuru karmāṇi saṅgaṁ tyaktvā dhanañjaya
siddhy-asiddhyoḥ samo bhūtvā samatvaṁ yoga uchyate

49

dūreṇa hy-avaraṁ karma buddhi-yogād dhanañjaya
buddhau śharaṇam anvichchha kṛipaṇāḥ phala-hetavaḥ

50

buddhi-yukto jahātīha ubhe sukṛita-duṣhkṛite
tasmād yogāya yujyasva yogaḥ karmasu kauśhalam

51

karma-jaṁ buddhi-yuktā hi phalaṁ tyaktvā manīṣhiṇaḥ
janma-bandha-vinirmuktāḥ padaṁ gachchhanty-anāmayam

52

yadā te moha-kalilaṁ buddhir vyatitariṣhyati
tadā gantāsi nirvedaṁ śhrotavyasya śhrutasya cha

53

śhruti-vipratipannā te yadā sthāsyati niśhchalā
samādhāv-achalā buddhis tadā yogam avāpsyasi

54

arjuna uvācha
sthita-prajñasya kā bhāṣhā samādhi-sthasya keśhava
sthita-dhīḥ kiṁ prabhāṣheta kim āsīta vrajeta kim

55

śhrī bhagavān uvācha
prajahāti yadā kāmān sarvān pārtha mano-gatān
ātmany-evātmanā tuṣhṭaḥ sthita-prajñas tadochyate

56

duḥkheṣhv-anudvigna-manāḥ sukheṣhu vigata-spṛihaḥ
vīta-rāga-bhaya-krodhaḥ sthita-dhīr munir uchyate

57

yaḥ sarvatrānabhisnehas tat tat prāpya śhubhāśhubham
nābhinandati na dveṣhṭi tasya prajñā pratiṣhṭhitā

58

yadā sanharate chāyaṁ kūrmo 'ṅgānīva sarvaśhaḥ
indriyāṇīndriyārthebhyas tasya prajñā pratiṣhṭhitā

59

vishayā vinivartante nirāhārasya dehinaḥ
rasa-varjaṁ raso 'pyasya paraṁ dṛishṭvā nivartate

60

yatato hyapi kaunteya puruṣhasya vipaśhchitaḥ
indriyāṇi pramāthīni haranti prasabhaṁ manaḥ

61

tāni sarvāṇi sanyamya yukta āsīta mat-paraḥ
vaśhe hi yasyendriyāṇi tasya prajñā pratiṣhṭhitā

62

dhyāyato vishayān puṁsaḥ saṅgas teṣhūpajāyate
saṅgāt sañjāyate kāmaḥ kāmāt krodho 'bhijāyate

63

krodhād bhavati sammohaḥ sammohāt smṛiti-vibhramaḥ
smṛiti-bhranśhād buddhi-nāśho buddhi-nāśhāt praṇaśhyati

64

rāga-dveṣha-viyuktais tu vishayān indriyaiśh charan
ātma-vaśhyair-vidheyātmā prasādam adhigachchhati

65

prasāde sarva-duḥkhānāṁ hānir asyopajāyate
prasanna-chetaso hyāśhu buddhiḥ paryavatiṣhṭhate

66

nāsti buddhir-ayuktasya na chāyuktasya bhāvanā
na chābhāvayataḥ śhāntir aśhāntasya kutaḥ sukham

67

indriyāṇāṁ hi charatāṁ yan mano 'nuvidhīyate
tadasya harati prajñāṁ vāyur nāvam ivāmbhasi

68

tasmād yasya mahā-bāho nigṛihītāni sarvaśhaḥ
indriyāṇīndriyārthebhyas tasya prajñā pratiṣhṭhitā

69

yā niśhā sarva-bhūtānāṁ tasyāṁ jāgarti sanyamī
yasyāṁ jāgrati bhūtāni sā niśhā paśhyato muneḥ

70

āpūryamāṇam achala-pratiṣhṭhaṁ
samudram āpaḥ praviśhanti yadvat
tadvat kāmā yaṁ praviśhanti sarve
sa śhāntim āpnoti na kāma-kāmī

71

vihāya kāmān yaḥ sarvān pumānśh charati niḥspṛihaḥ
nirmamo nirahankāraḥ sa śhāntim adhigachchhati

72

eṣhā brāhmī sthitiḥ pārtha naināṁ prāpya vimuhyati
sthitvāsyām anta-kāle 'pi brahma-nirvāṇam ṛichchhati

Contact

9839093003

myrichindia@gmail.com

facebook.com/drjagadeeshpillaiofficial

youtube.com/drjagadeeshpillai